OUR WILDLIFE WORLD

CROCODILES

Peter Carver

Grolier

FACTS IN BRIEF

Classification of Crocodiles

Class: *Reptilia* (reptiles)
Order: *Crocodilia* (crocodilians)
Family: *Crocodylidae* (crocodile family)
Genus: There are 3 genera of crocodiles.
Species: There are 14 species of crocodiles.

World distribution.   Tropical regions in southern North America, Central and South America, Asia, Africa, Madagascar, Australia and islands in the western Pacific Ocean.

Habitat.   Rivers, lakes, swamps and wetlands, and open salt water

Distinctive physical characteristics.   Dark green, gray or black skin; short legs with webbed feet and large powerful tail; ears and nostrils located on upper surface of long narrow head; even when closed, jaws show almost all teeth.

Habits.   Solitary or, during feeding and breeding, in groups dominated by large male. Basks on sandy or muddy banks near water's edge. Female buries eggs in sand or builds nest of leaves and mud.

Diet.   Fish, birds and mammals.

Published originally as
"Getting to Know . . . Nature's Children."

This series is approved and recommended by the Federation of Ontario Naturalists.

Canadian Cataloguing in Publication Data

Carver, Peter, 1936–
  Crocodiles

(Our wildlife world)
ISBN 0-7172-2657-3

1. Crocodiles—Juvenile literature.
I. Title.   II. Series.
QL666.C925C3   1990   j597.98   C90-095093-5

Contents

Long ago in Egypt the crocodile was considered holy. Temples were built in honor of gods pictured with crocodile heads, and the people even named one of their cities Crocodilopolos. Sacred crocodiles were kept in captivity, bedecked with gold bracelets and fed special food. When they died they were embalmed and wrapped in cloth as mummies, just like the great pharaohs, or kings, who were buried in the Pyramids.

Although crocodiles are no longer treated this way, people still find them both fascinating and terrifying. And they still cling to many mistaken notions about their habits and behavior. Let's try to find out what these mysterious and misunderstood creatures are really like.

Ancient Crocodiles

Crocodilian is the name given to a group of reptiles that includes crocodiles, alligators, gavials and caimans. Crocodilians have been around for a long time. They first appeared on the Earth more than 200 million years ago during a time known as the Age of Dinosaurs or the Age of Reptiles. The largest grew to be 15 metres (50 feet) long and probably snacked on dinosaurs.

Although dinosaurs eventually died out as climates changed and entire continents shifted, crocodilians survived. One reason may have been that they were able to hunt both on land and in the water. This gave them more flexibility when food became scarce. Surprisingly the crocodilians that exist today are very similar to their ancient ancestors.

*This crocodile is known as the
false gavial because of its long
narrow snout and its diet of fish.*

Reptile Relatives

Crocodiles, alligators, caimans and gavials all have a long snout filled with teeth, short legs, a long tail and thick scaly skin. So how do you tell one crocodilian from another? Mainly by the shape of their snout and where they live.

Gavials, or gharials as scientists prefer to call them, live in large rivers in India. They have 100 small teeth and a very narrow snout, that is the perfect shape for catching fish and frogs. They are one of the largest crocodilians, reaching a length of 7 metres (23 feet). Most caimans are much smaller than gavials and they have a broad snout. They are found in rivers, lakes and swamps from Mexico to Argentina.

Of all the crocodilians, alligators and crocodiles are the ones people tend to hear more about and are most likely to confuse. However, crocodiles are generally more active than alligators, and they have a narrower head and a more pointed snout. If you still aren't sure which is which, take a look at their teeth. Most of a crocodile's teeth are visible even when its mouth is closed. And you might notice that the extra

Alligator

Crocodile

large fourth tooth on either side of its lower jaw fits into a notch on the *outside* of its upper jaw. The alligator also has two enlarged teeth in its lower jaw, but they fit into a special hole *inside* its mouth and can't be seen when its mouth is closed. The ranges of the crocodile and the alligator overlap only in southern Florida.

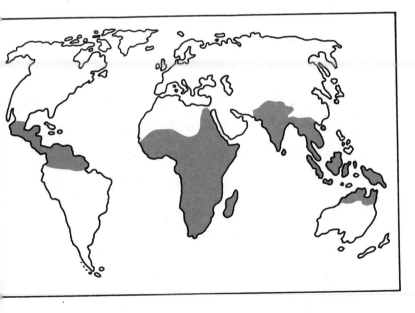

The shaded areas on this map show where crocodiles can be found.

Cold-Blooded Creatures

A crocodile is a reptile—but what's a reptile? Reptiles include animals such as snakes, turtles and lizards. They have a backbone—unlike creatures like worms—and they breathe air. Many spend part of their lives in water, but they must come to the surface to breathe. They also have dry scaly skin.

Another characteristic of reptiles is that they lay eggs from which their young hatch. Female reptiles go onto the land to lay their eggs. Unlike amphibians, whose young have a larval stage, reptile offspring develop directly. In fact, many types look exactly like small versions of their parents when they hatch.

Crocodiles, like other reptiles, are cold-blooded. This doesn't mean that their blood is actually cold but just that the temperature of their blood adjusts to the temperature of their surroundings. Crocodiles live in warm climates, so it is fairly easy for them to keep their bodies at a comfortable temperature level.

Soaking up the sun.

Crocodiles are considered the world's most intelligent reptiles. (Pygmy crocodile)

All Kinds of Crocodiles

There are 14 species of crocodiles living in the world today. Most live near fresh water or brackish swampy waters near sea coasts. They prefer slow-moving shallow water to large lakes or the open sea. Crocodiles are found in tropical regions in southern North America, Central and South America, Asia, Africa, Australia and islands in the western Pacific Ocean.

Crocodiles range in size from 8 metres (26 feet) to dwarf varieties that grow to be just over a metre (not quite 4 feet) long. The Indopacific, or saltwater, crocodile is the largest member of the family and also the largest reptile in the world. It is also the only type that will swim far out to sea—up to 1000 kilometres (600 miles). The smallest crocodiles are the West African and Congo dwarf crocodiles that inhabit tropical forests in Western Africa. The best-known variety is the Nile crocodile. It grows to be over 5 metres (16.5 feet) long and may weigh almost a tonne. It lives in most parts of Africa except in the Sahara and northwest areas.

Champion Swimmers

Opposite page:
You could never win a swimming race with a Johnston's crocodile — it's too fast.

Water is where crocodiles feel most at home. It's where they raise their young, feed and spend long hours quietly floating around.

The crocodile's body is perfectly suited to life in the water. Its short stubby legs aren't used for swimming, but are tucked close to its sides. It moves forward swiftly by swinging its long powerful tail from side to side. Its eyes and nostrils are on top of its head, so it can remain motionless in the water while still being able to see and breathe. When crocodiles dive underwater they close their nostrils and special ear flaps to keep out the water. And they are excellent at holding their breath—they can stay submerged for 30 minutes at a time.

Since crocodiles don't have any lips, water flows into their mouth when they are underwater. However, they don't have to worry about swallowing it because they have a special valve in their throat. This valve can be closed off so that water will not flow into their breathing passages. It also allows them to hold prey in their jaws or even eat underwater.

The Race Is On

Even though crocodiles spend a large part of their lives in water, they have been known to cover quite long distances overland. Nile crocodiles, for instance, have been seen up to 10 kilometres (6 miles) from the nearest river or swamp. Such journeys are made to find food or new bodies of water when their previous swimming hole has dried up. A crocodile on land looks clumsy, but in fact, it moves quite efficiently on its thick strong legs, and its webbed feet keep it from sinking into the mud.

Crocodiles move at four different speeds on land. Most often they can be seen slithering from riverbanks into the water on their bellies when they've been disturbed. However, their squat legs are strong enough to support their entire body and allow them to walk with their belly completely off the ground, although their tail does drag along behind. More surprisingly, a crocodile can run—and run faster than a human being over a short distance. One crocodile—Johnston's crocodile of northern Australia—has actually been known to *gallop.*

Opposite page:
A Nile crocodile venturing out onto land.

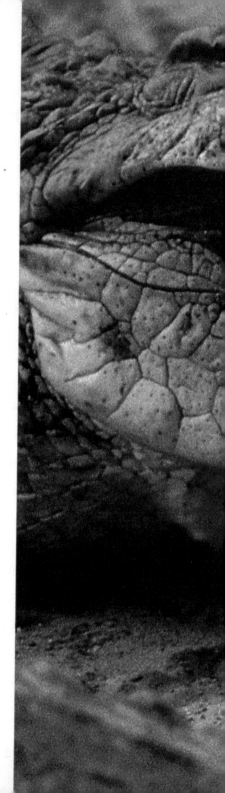

Open Wide

How many teeth do you think a crocodile has? If you said between 60 and 80 you're absolutely right. And when one tooth falls out another soon grows in its place.

A crocodile with its mouth wide open is a frightening sight. But you might be amazed to learn that its cone-shaped teeth aren't especially sharp and are of no use for chewing. Thanks to the crocodile's super-strong jaw muscles, however, they make an excellent weapon against intruders and are perfect for catching hold of and tearing prey. If the prey is small enough a crocodile will simply swallow it whole.

If you are close enough to count a crocodile's teeth, you are much too close!

Feeding Time

The crocodile is a skillful hunter. It floats just below the surface of the water with only its nostrils and eyes showing. It can stay so still that it is often mistaken for a log... until a fish, a bird or an animal is within reach. Then, snap! The great jaws open and clamp shut on the unsuspecting prey. It's almost impossible to pry open those jaws if the crocodile wants to keep them shut because of its powerful muscles.

Some crocodiles wait in the water where they know animals will come to drink. Then they grasp the animal by its nose or front legs or use a well-aimed swat of their tail to knock it into the water. Small prey is eaten immediately, while large prey is pulled deep into the water and kept there till it drowns.

What does a crocodile consider a delicious meal? Well, it wouldn't turn up its snout at much. It likes all kinds of fish, birds and mammals. In fact, it will eat just about anything it can catch—if it's hungry that is. Crocodiles don't usually feed every day and they will ignore their usual prey if they have a full stomach.

Opposite page:
Watching . . . and waiting . . .

Lazy Lifestyle

In general, the crocodile has a relaxed lifestyle. Most types hunt during the night. As soon as the sun comes up, they climb out of the water and find a comfortable spot to lie in the sunshine and soak up the rays. You may have seen photos of crocodiles on land with their mouths open. They aren't angry or hungry as you might expect, they are just a little bit too warm. By opening their mouth they are able to release excess moisture and heat, just as a dog does when it pants.

While relaxing in the sun, crocodiles in some areas may be visited by a small bird called an oxpecker. It perches on the back of the large reptile and then proceeds to peck bugs and any other creatures from its skin. While the crocodile sunbathes it gets a good cleaning as well.

A panting Cuban crocodile and a cooler companion.

Special Skin

The skin of the crocodile is designed for its watery lifestyle. Its thick hide helps to keep the water out. The dark brownish black color of the crocodile's skin helps it to absorb as much sunlight and warmth as possible. It also allows the crocodile to blend into the swampy surroundings it generally prefers.

Unfortunately as well as helping the crocodile to survive, its skin has almost brought about its extinction in certain areas. The scaly belly skin is highly valued as leather to make shoes, handbags, wallets and belts. So many crocodiles were killed for their skin that all species were at one time considered endangered. This situation has improved somewhat since crocodiles are now protected in many parts of the world.

A close up of a crocodile's scaly skin.

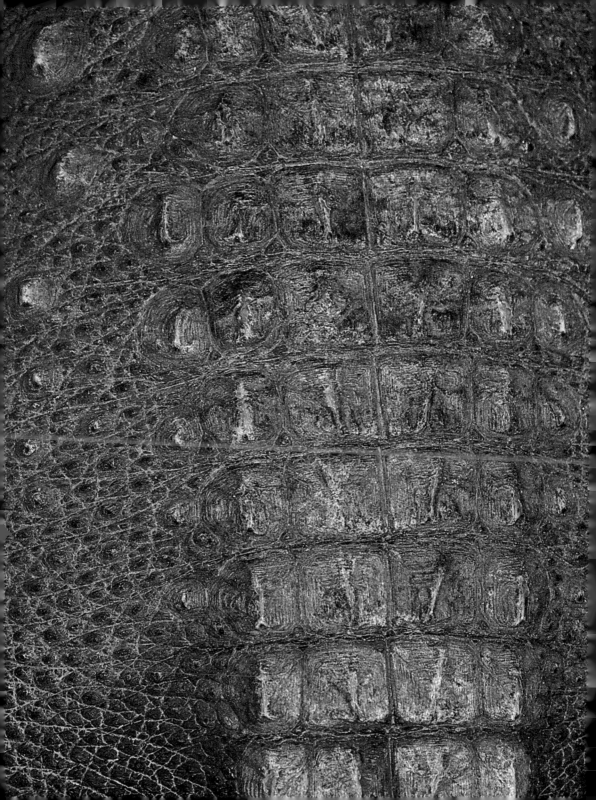

Sights and Sounds

Crocodiles are active at night, and like many other nocturnal animals they have eyes with vertical slit-shaped pupils. These widen in the dark to let in as much light as possible. Inside their eyes is a special reflective material—which your pet cat also has—to make use of all the available light.

Like many other animals that do a lot of diving or spend a lot of time in the water, the crocodile has an extra set of transparent eyelids. By closing them, it can protect its eyes underwater and still see fairly well.

The crocodile has excellent hearing and may rely on it for hunting even more than on its eyesight. Its ears are located on top of its head right behind its eyes. They are able to hear even the smallest sound when the crocodile is lying motionless in the water.

Crocodiles also have a well-developed sense of smell.

Saltwater crocodile.

Let's Talk

You might wonder how crocodiles communicate with one another. They make a number of noises, each of which means something different. An angry crocodile hisses, especially a female guarding her nest. During mating season, romantic couples grunt at each other to show affection. A crocodile defending its territory roars while spraying water in all directions. Neighbors will answer with roars of their own. Young crocodiles chirp or grunt softly at their mother and squeak or squeal when they're in danger. And sometimes crocodiles have been known to bark, although no one is certain just what that means.

Like many animals, crocodiles also communicate with body language. A raised head, a thrashing tail, a long measuring look all send messages that other crocodiles are quick to understand.

It doesn't take a crocodile expert to figure out that this crocodile is warning you to back off.

A pair of young Nile crocodiles cruising.

Keep Out

Crocodiles are solitary reptiles for the most part. Almost all types prefer to live on their own. Each crocodile has a territory that includes both land area and water that it defends from other crocodiles. Female territories, however, may overlap those of the males.

An adult may have the same territory for years unless the water dries up or there isn't enough food. Young crocodiles may have to relocate several times if a larger and older crocodile decides to take over their area.

A loud roar is usually all that is needed to warn an intruder to leave another crocodile's territory. Rarely will a crocodile actually have to defend its area by using its powerful jaws.

Nile crocodiles are unusual because they don't have separate territories except during mating season. They spend much of their time in groups basking on riverbanks together and searching for schools of fish to eat. Johnston's crocodiles may also gather together during the dry season when deep pools may be few and far between.

Getting Together

Somewhere between the ages of five and ten a crocodile mates for the first time. During the mating season large older males stake out an area and allow only females and young males to share it. They defend this territory fiercely from competing males and in the rare cases where a rival persists, fighting may continue until the death of one or the other.

A male shows he is interested in a female by swimming near her and splashing water around with his tail and snout. The couple then circle together, grunting at each other. Mating takes place in the water. They separate soon afterwards and the male does not take part in guarding the eggs or rearing the young.

Crocodile love.

*Female African crocodile guarding
her nest in a sandy riverbank.*

Watchful Mothers

Soon after mating the female crocodile builds a nest near the water. Usually the eggs are laid during the dry season so that the young will hatch during the wet season when food is plentiful. Some crocodiles lay their eggs in leaves to help keep them warm. Others bury them in the sand in a sunny spot. The female lays between 25 and 90 eggs that resemble long chicken eggs with shiny shells. Then she guards the nest, sometimes going without food. Lizards, birds, mongooses and even some crocodiles consider the eggs a tasty treat.

The eggs usually take three months to hatch. Just before hatching the crocodile mother hears squeaking and chirping sounds coming from the inside of the eggs. This is the signal for her to dig up the nest. Then she may carry the eggs to the water in her mouth, or she may wait until they hatch and lead her offspring to the water or carry them a few at a time in her mouth. The hatchlings break out of the egg using a small pointed egg tooth on the top of their snout. The tooth drops off soon after the baby hatches.

Hungry Hatchlings

The hatchlings are usually 15 to 25 centimetres (6 to 10 inches) long and they look like tiny versions of their parents. They are able to swim as soon as they enter the water. The next thing they do is to start eating. Breaking out of an egg is hard work and makes them hungry. The baby crocodiles begin by chasing and eating insects. Unlike most reptile mothers, the female crocodile watches over her young for the first few weeks of their lives, and in some cases for several months. Her offspring stay very close to her at the beginning. In fact, they usually crawl all over her head and body.

This is a dangerous time for young crocodiles because they have so many enemies and so few defences. Birds, fish and even adult crocodiles may gobble them up. They try to remain hidden as much as possible and rely on their mother for protection.

It's hatching day!

Hitching a ride. (Thailand crocodiles)

Bigger and Bigger

Young crocodiles soon progress from eating bugs to stalking frogs, fish and birds. In no time at all they are competent hunters. And little by little as they grow larger they are able to manage on their own.

For the first few years crocodiles grow about 30 centimetres (a foot) each year. After that they grow more slowly, but some keep growing all their lives. No one is sure exactly how long crocodiles can live. In captivity they have survived for up to 40 years, but scientists believe that a few of the giant ones in the wild may be over 100 years old!

Man-Eaters?

Crocodiles have a reputation for being ferocious man-eaters that will go out of their way to find a human being to devour. This is simply not true. Not too suprisingly, some of the largest varieties have been known to eat a human who happens along when they are hungry, and any crocodile will attack if it is cornered or if someone gets too close to its nesting site.

Most crocodiles, however, prefer to avoid contact with people altogether. Adult crocodiles have no natural predators. The only living thing that threatens them is man.

*Extreme caution should always be
used when crocodiles are nearby.*

Who Would Miss the Crocodile?

It is important for people to realize that crocodiles aren't evil creatures and that they play a significant and useful role in life in tropical regions. Enormous numbers of crocodiles are still being killed for their skin, and swamps are being filled in and changed into farmland, destroying their habitats. The resulting decrease in the crocodile population has already had an impact. For instance, Nile crocodiles eat large fish that prey upon the smaller fish that are an important food source for the people of the area. As the number of crocodiles decreases, the number of large fish increases and there are fewer small fish for people to catch and eat.

Fortunately people are coming to realize the important role crocodiles play in the world. They are protected by law in many countries, and reserves have been set up for them. As well, special farms are hatching crocodile eggs and then later returning the young to the wild. With conservation and better understanding, of them the outlook for these amazing reptiles is beginning to improve.

Relaxing after a hard day of hunting and sun bathing. (Mugger, or marsh crocodile)

Words to Know

Amphibians   A group of animals that live both on land and in water. Frogs, toads and salamanders are amphibians.

Cold-blooded   Term used for animals that have no automatic internal control of their body temperature.

Egg tooth   A tooth-like point on a crocodile's snout used to help it crack out of its egg.

Hatch   To emerge from an egg.

Hatchling   Newly hatched crocodile.

Mating season   Time during which animals come together to produce young.

Predator   An animal that hunts other animals for food.

Prey   Animal that other animals hunt for food.

Reptile   Class of cold-blooded animals that includes crocodiles, snakes, turtles and lizards.

Territory   Area that an animal or a group of animals lives in and often defends from animals of the same kind.

INDEX

Cover Photo: Australia Info Service

Photo Credits: Breck P. Kent, pages 4, 15, 16, 23, 24, 25, 31, 35, 43; Bill Ivy, pages 7, 12, 27; Four By Five inc., page 11; Robert Winslow, page 19; Christopher R. Harris (Shostal Associates), page 20; Tom McHugh (Photo Researchers, inc.), page 28; Tim Tuten (Black Star), page 32; Tony Dawson, page 36; New York Zoological Society, page 39; Phyllis Greenberg, page 40; G. Ziesler (Peter Arnold, inc.), page 45; Boyd Norton, page 46.